The Biz

By Ron Berman

Scobre Press Corporation
2255 Calle Clara
La Jolla, CA 92037

Scobre Press books may be purchased for
educational, business or sales promotional use.
First Scobre edition published 2008.

Edited by Charlotte Graeber
Cover Art & Layout by Michael Lynch
Content Editing & Research by Arica Rai Zimmerman

ISBN # 1-934713-14-7

HOME RUN EDITION

This story is based on the real life of Mark Mayfield, although
some names, quotes, and details of events have been altered.

The "Special Thanks Awards" go to:

Eric Conner
Starring as NYFA instructor

Alan Fiterman
Featured as director/NYFA instructor

Special appearance by Diane Wu
As "the intern"

Cameo appearances by
Snickers, Smokey, and Riley

And introducing Mark Mayfield ...
Actor, director, all-around awesome guy

and ... "Action!"

Chapter One

Hollywood

Isn't it amazing how technology has changed the world? As one newspaper said, "New inventions are having a big effect on the way people live. We can now work or play at almost any hour of the day or night! This new century is only a few years old, but it's going to be the most exciting time ever."

Wait ... you didn't think that newspaper was talking about right *now*, did you? Did you think it was talking about things like Wi-Fi, text messaging, and GPS? If you did, you would be wrong. Those words in the newspaper were written more than 100 years ago! They were talking about the *last* century.

Back then, people were very excited about new technology. It was the early 1900s, and electricity had just been invented. So had telephones, airplanes, cars, and hundreds of other things. They would change the world and the way we live.

One of these inventions would have a big influence on some of the things we do for fun. It was developed by Thomas Edison, who was a famous inventor. Mr. Edison called it the Kinetoscope. It was a camera that could record motion. Think of Mr. Edison's invention as the world's first video camera!

Early versions of the Kinetoscope were simple, and the quality wasn't very good. But it wasn't long before these cameras improved. Soon, they were able to create a good picture. The movie business was ready to take off.

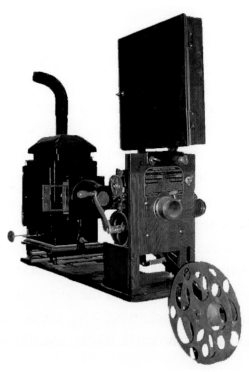

At first, most film directors worked in New York. Over time, some of them headed west to Los Angeles. That was the beginning of the modern movie age. But films were not made then like they are today. As a matter of fact, most of them were short films, or "shorts." Some of them lasted as little as 10 or 15 minutes.

Filmmakers continued to move to Los Angeles. They liked the good weather and friendly people. Something interesting happened, though. A tiny village near downtown LA ended up becoming even more popular. That village was called Hollywood.

People from all over the world are interested in Hollywood. That's why Los Angeles is such a popular vacation spot. Universal Studios provides a behind-the-scenes look at how movies are made. Grauman's Chinese Theater is another fun place. It's one of the most famous movie theaters in the world. If you go there, you'll see the actual handprints and footprints of hundreds of celebrities ... such as Adam Sandler and the cast of the *Harry Potter* movies.

Millions of visitors have enjoyed trips to Los Angeles over the years. They love the miles and miles of sandy beaches. What a perfect fit for a city that has bright sunshine all year long! After a relaxing day at the beach, many people go out to eat. In a big city like LA, there are many different types of restaurants. After a nice dinner, there's still more to do. Some people are lucky enough to have tickets to a Lakers game. They will hit the freeway and cruise to the Staples Center—joining celebrities such as Chris Rock, Denzel Washington, and Jack Nicholson.

It's very exciting to be in such a famous city. Tour buses take visitors through the streets of Beverly Hills. Tour guides point out which celebrities live in the mansions they pass. Another tourist hot spot is the Hollywood Wax Museum. It is home to hundreds of wax figures of movie stars, old and new.

The list of things to do in Los Angeles is endless. Some people try to spot a celebrity having a "power lunch" at The Ivy. A power lunch means talking about business while eating a fancy lunch. Hollywood business people often discuss the next movie a famous actor will star in. And The Ivy? It's the favorite restaurant of some of Hollywood's most important people. Photographers are usually standing across the street. They take pictures of celebrities who show up at The Ivy for lunch!

Besides the thousands of visitors, other people come to Los Angeles each year. Sure, they hope to see or meet a superstar. But that's not all. They also hope to *become* one. They are young actors and actresses, writers, directors, and producers. They want to get involved in the business of entertainment—which is known as *The Biz*.

A young actress poses at a photo shoot in LA. Is she the next big thing?

Making it in show business isn't easy. It's very different from a "normal" career, like being a doctor or a teacher. A young person who chooses one of those careers is in a good position. He or she can become successful by working hard and getting an education. The movie business doesn't work that way. It's not nearly as certain—there are no "sure things" in *The Biz*. The truth is that most people who chase this dream don't make it. They don't become movie stars or well-known directors.

But, anyone who has a dream in life should go for it. Most actors or directors want to become the next Will Smith or M. Night Shyamalan. But even for those who don't make it to that level, all is not lost. There are hundreds of other great careers in the movie business. They include everything from set design to stunt work. Many people who start out with the idea of becoming famous end up doing these jobs.

Thousands of teenagers across this country are preparing for a career in the movie business. One of them is Mark Mayfield, of Atlanta, Georgia. Mark has big dreams. That's why he's always writing a script, acting in a play, or directing a short film.

Besides being talented, Mark is also smart. He knows how tough the business is, even for someone with a lot of potential. That's why he has a plan for success. He is going to learn the movie business from top to bottom. Mark wants to be a famous actor and director. But he's also learning about those other jobs, such as lighting and film editing.

The sky's the limit for Mark, who just turned 18. His career is off to a flying start. He's already directed four short films! They show his unique view of the world.

Mark

Love All uses tennis as a background. It tells the story of a boy and girl who meet by chance.

Exposed is all about dealing with difficult situations. In the movie, Mark plays the role of a young filmmaker. With everything going wrong around him, he must learn to cope.

If the World Went Deaf is an interesting story. All of a sudden, people can no longer hear each other!

Finally, *Ruff Season* is very funny. It shows how each of us deals with frustration in our own way.

Besides the four films he's directed, Mark has also done a lot of other things. He's been involved in many other productions as an actor or a writer. That's in addition to the work he's done behind the scenes. It all fits into his plan to learn everything about the movie business.

The next step for Mark is to attend college. With a perfect 4.0 GPA, he's well on his way. "College will prepare me for life, as well as a career in the movie business. Then it will be time to take my shot out in Los Angeles."

Ah, yes, Los Angeles. For Mark, and many other people, that's where the dream begins. Once they get to LA, they're playing for real. They know it will be tough. There are many stories about people who try and fail. Sadly, some of them become discouraged and turn to alcohol and drugs.

That's not going to happen to a smart teenager like Mark. He isn't afraid to go for something that matters to him. And this *really* matters to him. Mark is shooting for a career in *The Biz*. He knows that there's only one place to make it happen: Hollywood.

He's already visited LA, and one day Mark will be back for good. He will make the trip from Atlanta to California to chase down his dreams. He's not the first person from the state of Georgia to do that. Julia Roberts did. So did Ryan Seacrest, Usher, Raven Symoné, Chris Tucker, and Ty Pennington. And too many more to even list. These celebrities were all either born in Georgia, or lived there at one time. Each of them, at some point in their life, headed west. They decided to take their chances in a magical land—a place where movies are made, TV shows are filmed, and dreams come true. They all headed to Hollywood.

Just like Mark will one day.

Chapter Two

The Director

Most people know that a director is the person who brings a movie to life. At first, the screenwriter puts the words down on paper. But he (or she) is not the one who turns those words into a movie. It's the director who does that. Of course, without actors there wouldn't even be movies. But the director tells the actors *how* to perform some of the scenes. He also decides what camera angles to shoot from, and what music will be in the film.

That's just the beginning. Directors make most of the decisions, even the small ones. They decide what clothes the actors wear, and how the credits roll at the end of the movie. Because the actors are more famous, they are the ones that people talk about. Still, it's the director who actually creates a movie. As one film teacher says, "The director is God. The entire movie is made from his or her ideas."

Many directors are also famous. Steven Spielberg, Martin Scorsese, Peter Jackson. How about Penny Marshall, Spike Lee, or Sofia Coppola? These men and women have directed films like *Jaws*, *Goodfellas*, the *Lord of the Rings* trilogy, *A League of Their Own*, *Inside Man*, and *Lost in Translation*.

How cool are movies? For almost 100 years, they have entertained us. When we're watching a good movie, we become totally involved in the story. It may simply be funny and make us laugh. Or, we may enter a make-believe world, where sorcerers and hobbits live. In some cases, it's all about the action of car chases and police shoot-outs. We all have our favorites, which is why there are so many different kinds of movies. It's the job of the director to make it all come together.

There are many benefits to being a director. They make movies that can influence people all over the world. After all, sometimes films are more than just pure entertainment. They can also talk about politics, or even teach people about new hobbies—such as

Dogtown and Z-Boys, and *Riding Giants*. Those films are about the exciting sports of skateboarding and big-wave surfing.

All directors enjoy making movies and telling great stories. Some of them even win an Academy Award. That is definitely one of Mark Mayfield's goals. He's been dreaming about the movie business for a long time.

Like many creative people, Mark has a lot of imagination. It's been that way ever since childhood. His mind will wander once in a while, sometimes even during school. He will look out the window and daydream about villains standing outside. "I suddenly become a superhero, whose job is to defeat the bad guys," he laughs.

Creative and fun ... Mark at age 13.

It's easy to see why Mark fell in love with TV and movies. When he was young, his family would go to the movie theater once a week. It started with Disney films. Later on, Mark started liking movies such as the *Lord of the Rings* trilogy. It didn't even matter what film was playing. A trip to the movie theater was always fun. "I just loved being there, especially for a movie that everybody was talking about," Mark remembers. "As a matter of fact, I still love it."

Mark also started noticing how films tell great stories. This was the beginning of his career as a director. He didn't realize it at the time, of course. All he knew was that a good story gave him strong feelings. "I like anything that is creative, but to me nothing is more powerful than film. I think maybe it's because it brings so many things together—music, writing, and photography."

Mark was so into TV and movies that he used to go straight home every day after school. He enjoyed watching TV more than playing outside. After a while, he went back to playing sports and hanging out with his friends. But by then he had decided that he wanted to be involved with movies. He wanted to be more than just a fan.

At first, Mark wanted to be an actor. However, there was one big problem: He felt nervous, and even a little scared. He worried that he wouldn't be good enough. "I think I've always been a somewhat insecure guy," he admits. "I don't know why, but I'm pretty good at freaking myself out about stuff."

He's not alone. People often get worried when they are in difficult situations. It's tough to deal with preparing for an upcoming test or trying to make new friends. However, a good lesson comes from the film *A Cinderella Story*: "Don't let the fear of striking out keep you from playing the game." Still, Mark struggled with his fears for a long time. He wasn't sure he would ever be able to stand on a stage and be an actor.

In the summer of 2005, Mark went to tennis camp. Over the years, tennis had become his best sport. Days at camp were spent playing tennis under the hot Florida sun. At night, however, fun classes and programs were made available to campers.

Mark decided to sign up for a program called "Game On." One of the classes in the program was "improv." That's short for "improvisation." Improv means making something up and acting it out. Here's an example: You and your friend pretend to be on a boat in the middle of a lake, fishing. You might talk about how relaxing it is to hang out on a boat. You could also act out a funny skit about catching a huge fish. The goal is to make it interesting, especially if there's an audience watching. Improv isn't easy because you're always being put on the spot. That's the whole point, though. You learn how to deal with situations where you have to come up with something to say. This is good training for job interviews, or even going out on a date!

Mark was very nervous when he first tried improv. But once he got going, he found that he enjoyed it very much. "The main thing improv taught me was that I can overcome my fears," he says. That important lesson changed Mark's life. He was 15 years old, about to turn 16, and becoming more confident. He felt like he was finally ready to do what he was meant to do.

When Mark returned home from tennis camp, he jumped online right away. He started chatting with Claire McCleskey, an actress and good friend. Later, another friend, Sarah Walker, came online. Mark told them all about the summer: the tennis matches he had played, and the new friends he had made. He saved the best for last, though. He had a surprise for them…

Although Mark was into movies, it wasn't something he talked about as a career. In fact, most people thought he might become a veterinarian. As an animal lover, this made a lot of sense. But his lack of confidence had been stopping him from doing what he *truly* wanted to do. This was no longer the case. Mark dropped the news. He told Claire and Sarah all about the Game On program and the improv classes. He let them know that he had made a huge decision: He was going to be an actor.

Mark has had pets his whole life. This photo shows him at age 11 with his dog, Snickers.

Chapter Three

Impressive Debut

A few weeks after tennis camp, school started up again. Mark signed up for a class called "Introduction to Theater." He was now a sophomore at Westminster High School in Atlanta. He was pumped up, and ready to tackle a new challenge.

This was an amazing change in Mark. Remember, he had once been too shy to even tell anyone he wanted to be an actor. Now, he decided to audition for a one-act play called *The Stone Guest*. To his surprise, he earned a role in it. He couldn't believe how quickly things were happening. After two months of rehearsal, Mark was ready to perform for the first time ever. It was November of 2005—less than four months since he had taken the improv class at tennis camp.

A few minutes before the show started, Mark peeked out from behind the curtains. It was a packed house! The auditorium was filled with his family and all his friends.

Mark was feeling the pressure. He was so nervous that he felt sick. He was suffering from a case of stage fright. That's something that most performers can relate to.

As the lights went down and the music began, people stared at the stage. Mark was still nervous, but he walked out to the center of the stage. He gave a good performance. It wasn't perfect, but it was an impressive debut. When the play was over, he received a standing ovation. It made him feel great. "As soon as I heard that applause, I knew this was what I wanted to do," he says. "I want to connect with people. That's what acting and making movies are all about."

Since that time, Mark has written and performed in many high school productions. He's done it all, including comedy, drama, and dancing and singing in musicals.

Getting ready for a performance backstage.

Mark made a smart choice in becoming an actor. First of all, it's something he loves. But it's also a great way to learn things that will make him a better director. Most directors have never been famous actors, but many are. In fact, some of them continue to act when they are not directing a film. This is what Mark wants to do. Clint Eastwood is a good example, because he's the star of more than 100 films. He also won the 2004 Academy Award for Best Director for his film *Million Dollar Baby*.

Another good example is Spike Lee. He often appears in the movies he directs. This goes back more than 20 years to his first film, *She's Gotta Have It*. Oliver Stone is the director of famous films such as *Any Given Sunday* and *JFK*. He's also made "cameos" in some of his own movies. A cameo is when somebody shows up in a film as a surprise. For example, in *Wedding Crashers*, Will Ferrell suddenly popped up on the screen. Fans enjoyed his small, but funny, role.

Mark's career will lead him in many exciting directions. Still, he will always love epics and fantasy tales. *The Lord of the Rings: The Fellowship of the Ring* and *X-Men* are two of his favorites. He's also very much into films such as *Bicentennial Man* and *Forrest Gump*. These movies show what it means to be a person with real feelings. "I can see making those types of films in the future," Mark says. "My stories won't always have bloody battles or flashy powers— although I love that stuff, too."

When Mark was younger, he didn't think about *how* a movie is made. "I just knew that I wanted to be involved in movies," he says. "It started out with acting. Then, after a while, I realized that I wanted to be in control of the entire film."

It was exciting to think about, but Mark was also worried. There are many ways to tell a story. That makes it a huge challenge for the director. "I always wondered if I could do it," Mark says. "I saw things very clearly in my mind. I didn't know if I would be able to get them on the screen that way."

For a long time, Mark thought about it. He wasn't sure if directing was the right career for him. Yet, whenever he saw a fantastic movie, he got fired up. There was one thing he knew for sure: He wanted to create his own stories and share them with people. That's how many directors feel. They have the desire to connect with people through the movies they make.

Making a great movie isn't easy, though. Mark was still nervous about whether or not he could really do it. He's thankful that he had a deep moment one day while sitting in a theater. It was one of those moments you remember because it changes your life.

With a laugh, Mark explains what happened. It wasn't an amazing movie that gave him the inspiration to follow his dreams. As a matter of fact, it was the complete opposite. He and a friend went to see a new movie by a well-known director.

Mark had been looking forward to this film very much. Based on the previews, it seemed like it would be awesome. However, sometimes previews can be misleading. "The movie totally *sucked*," Mark says with a smile. "My friend and I couldn't even believe it!"

This was Mark's eye-opening moment. As he sat in the theater, his mind was racing. He thought about his own life and goals. "I was like, 'Dude, this famous director just made a lame movie. And a lot of people will go and see it. I *know* I can make a better one, so why not?'"

Filmmaking was something that Mark loved and wanted to do. He knew that it was time to put the doubts aside. He was very pleased as he walked out of the theater with his friend. Instead of being mad that he wasted time and money on a bad movie, he felt good. With a laugh, he says, "I *really* enjoyed watching a bad movie that day. It was the best thing for my career!"

Many thanks to that director for making such a lousy movie. And for helping Mark Mayfield get on the road to making many great ones.

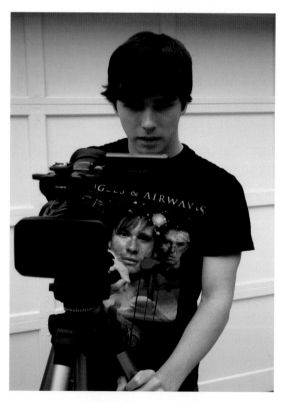

Mark at work, making sure that the scene is perfect.

Chapter Four

Right Place, Right Time

Mark's heart suddenly started beating fast. *Very* fast. Jason La Padura was standing less than 20 feet from him! Mark whispered to his friend Ari Grabb, "Dude, that guy is the casting director for *Heroes*."

"Are you sure?" Ari asked. He blinked a few times to adjust his eyes to the bright California sun.

"Trust me, I'm sure," Mark answered. This was the kind of information only a guy like Mark would know. After all, *Heroes* is one of his favorite TV shows. The exciting drama became a big hit in 2006, its very first season. The show is about people who have special powers that affect the fate of the world.

Mark had every reason to be excited about seeing a Hollywood casting director. This is a very important job. Every TV show and movie has to select, or "cast," actors for different roles. That's what the casting director does. It's like an employer deciding whom to hire for a job.

Most people don't give it much thought, but casting is a very creative job. Consider a young Lindsay Lohan in *Freaky Friday*—or a *freaky* killer in the 2008 Academy Award-winning Best Picture *No Country for Old Men*. (That role was played by Javier

Bardem.) Casting directors always try to find the right actor for each role.

The process often begins with a "casting call." That's a way of making people aware that a role is available. Usually this information reaches agents or managers. They set up auditions for the actors they represent. On the day of the audition, actors come in and "read." That means that they perform a few lines of the script.

In an audition, the actor tries to *become* the person he would be playing on the screen. That might mean using a fake limp, or talking like someone from a different country. He wants to be believable as that character. If he is, the casting directors will be impressed. As an example, an actor might read for the role of a juvenile delinquent. He will try to look and sound convincing as a kid from the "street."

If you were the casting director, which actor would you choose?

When all the auditions are finished, the casting directors have a lot to think about. They have to use their judgment. There's no way to *prove* that somebody is right (or wrong) for a part. They have to figure out which actor can give the best performance.

The director of a film is also involved in the casting process. Once in a while, he will already have someone in mind for one of the leading roles. Some directors and stars find so much success as a team that they continue working together. Tim Burton has directed Johnny Depp in six films. Another famous team is Martin Scorsese and Leonardo DiCaprio. They have made three films together, including 2007's Academy Award-winning *The Departed*.

If the director doesn't have a favorite actor, the casting call goes out. There is almost always a big response. As many as 100 people or more may show up to audition, even for one small role. It's always a tough choice for the casting directors. They usually film the auditions so they can watch some of them later. Sometimes they're simply not sure whom to cast. In those cases, they might ask one or more of the actors to audition again. This is known as a "callback."

Most actors audition for roles through casting calls. That's the way things are normally done. But there's nothing normal about Hollywood. It truly is an unpredictable town. Maybe that's why some people refer to it as "Holly-*weird*." Sometimes things can happen unexpectedly. They sure did for Mark on this day in July of 2007. He suddenly found himself in the right place at the right time.

This was only Mark's second trip to Los Angeles. Yet there he was, staring at the casting director of his favorite TV show! Many people wouldn't even recognize the stars of *Heroes*. How many would recognize the casting director? Big ups to Mark for being on top of this type of information.

In Hollywood, there's a long history of things like this happening. In some cases, they have helped careers move forward. Everyone knows Harrison Ford as the star of the *Indiana Jones* movies, *Star Wars*, *Air Force One*, *The Fugitive*, and several other hits. But he was a carpenter before he struck gold as an actor. That's right—a carpenter—as in someone who builds stuff with tools. A lucky thing happened to Ford once. George Lucas, a famous director, hired him to build some cabinets for his home. Three years later, Harrison Ford was cast as Han Solo in *Star Wars*— directed by George Lucas!

Mark quickly jumped at *his* opportunity. He cleared his throat and wiped his sweaty hands. Then he walked up to Mr. La Padura and introduced himself. Mark explained that he was an actor and director from Atlanta. As they talked about *Heroes*, Mark impressed Mr. La Padura. It was clear that Mark knew everything about the show. Then he dropped the question on his mind.

"Have you already cast the role of Claire's boyfriend for the upcoming season?" Mark asked. He tried to sound casual as he spoke.

For those who aren't fans of the show, Claire is a beautiful high school student. That's not all. She also has the amazing ability to heal from any injury—even falling from a tall building or getting shot! Mark figured that his best chance to get cast on the show might be as Claire's boyfriend.

Mr. La Padura explained that they were all set for the current season. Luckily, though, they hadn't yet cast the part for future seasons. He invited Mark to drop off his "headshot" directly to Mr. La Padura's attention. A headshot is an 8x10 photo that actors use to advertise themselves. Mark was very happy about it. Sure, that didn't guarantee anything. Still, it was like a baseball player being invited to try out for the New York Yankees!

Hopefully, Mr. La Padura remembers this headshot!

Maybe you'll see Mark Mayfield on *Heroes* in future seasons. If so, you'll have the inside scoop on how it happened. But as Mark will tell you, he's not counting on it. "You never expect to get any one role," he explains. "It's about trying to create lots of opportunities for yourself. If you do, sooner or later something is going to hit. If it's not *Heroes*, maybe it will be the next thing."

Mark makes a good point. Some people just sit around and wait for their phone to ring. That's just not the way it works in Hollywood. Sometimes it takes years, but an actor has to be out there, "networking." That's a word that means meeting new people who can help your career.

"Meeting the casting director of *Heroes* was awesome," Mark says. "In Hollywood, it's important to work hard and keep a positive attitude. It may take a long time, but I *will* get where I want to go."

On Mark's last night in LA, he takes in a quiet and reflective moment at the beach. In his heart, he knows he'll be back.

Chapter Five

Before the Cameras Start Rolling

What is the process of making a movie? As Mark explains, it can take a long time. A film is only truly finished when people are sitting in the theater watching it. Only then has all that hard work paid off for the director and the actors—and everybody else who was involved in making the movie.

The next time you're sitting in a theater enjoying a movie, stop for a moment. Think about what it took to get it there. That film probably began several *years* earlier. The starting point could have been a great book (such as J. K. Rowling's *Harry Potter*). Or, maybe it was a script that somebody at a movie studio really liked. These are only a couple of possibilities. There are plenty more.

Many things have to happen before the cameras start rolling. Hollywood is all about making deals. This brings us to the role of the producer. It is one of the most important careers in the movie business. As long as there have been movies, there have been producers. They get involved in every part of making a movie.

Smiles all around: A slick young agent shakes hands with a powerful movie producer. He has just made a multimillion-dollar deal on behalf of his movie-star client.

Some producers are famous. The movies *American Gangster*, *Flightplan*, *Cinderella Man*, and *Blue Crush* have something in common: They were all produced by a Hollywood legend named Brian Grazer.

The producer is usually the first person that gets involved with a "project." That's a Hollywood word that means a movie. Take Brian Grazer, for instance. Famous producers like him are always being sent scripts to read. They also go to meetings where agents and managers "pitch" their projects. (Pitch is yet another Hollywood word. It means trying to convince someone else about how good an idea or script is.)

Imagine that one day Mr. Grazer is given a script by one of his writer friends. The movie is called *Outer Space War*. After reading the script, Mr. Grazer is very impressed. "It's awesome," he tells his friend. "I'm having lunch at The Ivy next week with Tobey Maguire's agent. I'll pitch the idea of having Tobey play the hero who saves the world—just like he did in *Spider-Man*. His agent will flip!"

It's very helpful to have someone with Brian Grazer's influence in the mix. He can pitch a script to the big Hollywood movie studios. They have the millions of dollars it takes to make this type of big-budget film. Then Mr. Grazer will line up a famous director. He'll also start talking directly with the agents of some other movie stars.

The more people that sign on to the film, the better it is. That makes it easier for a producer to strike a deal with the studio. When a superstar like Tobey Maguire wants to star in a movie, it makes a huge difference. Knowing that, most studios would jump at the chance to get involved.

Of course, these things don't happen overnight. They can take months, or even years. There is also a great deal of business that takes place. Lawyers, managers, and agents are involved, in addition to the producer. But quite often this is how a movie gets started.

Once the director and actors are ready, filming begins. By then, the script is finished, and the cast and crew have all been hired. Some movies, such as *Napoleon Dynamite*, shoot in as little as 22 days. Other movies take longer. James Cameron's hit movie *Titanic* took around six months to be completed.

Money is always an important issue. Movie studios only spend millions of dollars if they feel a movie will be a hit. Obviously, they make money when people go to the theater to see the movie. There are also other ways to make a profit. They include rentals, downloads, and DVD purchases.

Will the film be a success? In Hollywood, it's always a roll of the dice.

Costs can be very different for each film. *Napoleon Dynamite* was shot for less than a million dollars. *Titanic*, on the other hand, had a budget of $200 million! That makes it one of the most expensive films of all time. Yet, it *still* made a huge profit.

A camera crew on a Spike Lee film in New York.

As a movie is filmed, hundreds of people are involved. There are many jobs for people who are interested in the movie business. They include building the sets, doing hair and makeup, and making lunch for the cast and crew. These are only a few of the jobs that are available. After all, every detail has to be covered, even down to hiring animal trainers. (Consider how many films feature a dog, a cat, or even a grizzly bear!)

An actress gets her hair and makeup done before an important scene.

Film editing is another good example. "You actually make a movie *three* times," Mark says. "The first time is when it's written. Then it's filmed, and finally edited." He's right, because things change each time. The filmed version usually comes out differently than the writer planned it. Then, the final edited version is different from the filmed version.

Some jobs are so unique that only a handful of people are trained to do them. Almost everyone has watched a movie in which the main star does something incredible. Sometimes it's jumping from a moving car, while other times it's a high-speed chase. However, it's usually not the star that is risking injury. Instead, a stunt double takes his place.

High-speed chase: A stuntman hits insane speeds while standing in for an actor.

Another career in the movie business is art. This field also includes computers, science, and technology. In the movies, art combines everything from special effects to animation. It was used in the 1996 Will Smith summer hit *Independence Day*. In one scene, it looks like the White House is being blown to bits. Obviously that didn't really happen—special effects make it possible to trick the human eye.

There has always been a need for talented artists, going back more than 100 years. That's when animated films, or cartoons, were introduced. Things started taking off with the Disney character Mickey Mouse way back in 1928. Since then, cartoons and animation have always been a part of the movie business—and TV, of course. As a matter of fact, *The Simpsons* is the longest-running sitcom in American history.

Over the years, animation has improved a lot. Still, it's a long and careful process: More than four years were needed to complete the animation for *Shrek*. To put it all together, it takes skilled artists and people who are great with computers.

So those are some of the jobs that are part of *making* a movie. But what happens after a movie is completed? What makes a film a "hit?" Well, star power is certainly important. That's why superstar actors are paid millions of dollars. Haven't all of us gone to a movie simply because our favorite actor was in it?

Star power is not the only reason a film becomes a hit, though. Advertising and promoting a movie play a big role. Studios spend millions of dollars to promote a blockbuster movie. They do things like put up movie posters and have stars appear on talk shows. There is Internet buzz (like hyping the film on MySpace or Facebook), and ads on TV. Sometimes text messages are sent to thousands of cell phones. There is always an exciting "trailer" (short scenes from the movie to get people interested in it).

Many people choose careers in film advertising and promotion. They are usually young people who love business and movies. They go to college and earn a degree. That helps them get right in the middle of the movie business. They can make a lot of money, too.

Mark is very clear about the fact that he wants to either act in movies or direct them. However, he wants to leave all options open for the future. "I'm planning to get my degree no matter what," he says. "I've heard stories about people who were lucky enough to do one or two movies. But then, their careers sort of fell off."

Mark is smart. Getting his degree is an excellent idea. It will come in handy if one day he can't act or direct anymore. He'll have something to fall back on. He can always do something else in the movie business. As an example, he enjoys film editing. So a job like that would make perfect sense. He sums it up by saying, "One way or the other, I always want to be in *The Biz*."

Mark carefully looks over a script he's working on. Screenwriting is another career he is interested in.

Chapter Six

The Most Important Person on the Set

"Cut!"

Mark walked over to the actors, who were trying to get a scene just right. He had noticed that the actress kept pushing her hair to the side. Mark felt that this would distract the audience. More importantly, the actors didn't seem "natural" to him.

In the scene, the main character is in his apartment. There is a knock on the door. He opens it and invites his girlfriend to sit down on the couch. The problem was that the actors were stiff in the way they were moving. To overcome it, Mark explained what he wanted. He told the actors to walk past the kitchen, pause, and take a look around. Then they could keep walking to the couch. "Be natural, like you've taken this walk a thousand times," he said.

Mark explains how he wants the scene to unfold.

Finally, Mark was confident that the actors understood his directions. He then talked to the cinematographer. That's the person who holds the camera and actually shoots the film. Mark reminded him to shoot a wide shot at the beginning. Then, when the actors sat down on the couch, the camera could move in for a close-up.

"Places, everybody. Okay, quiet on the set, please ... and action!"

This time, the actors performed the scene much better. Mark was very pleased. He had only needed six "takes," or six attempts, to get it perfect. Still, it had taken a lot of time to set everything up and get the lighting just right. Mark had also made changes in what the actors were wearing, which slowed things down. Now, it was already almost noon. Mark called out to the cast and crew that they had a half-hour break for lunch.

Everyone quickly walked away, talking and laughing. The people who prepare lunch had set up a nice table of food. Mark didn't have time to eat, though. As the director, he had too many things to do.

Mark started thinking about the next scene he would be filming. He looked over the script and made some notes. He also exchanged some text messages with his "A.D." (Assistant Director). Finally, he called the producer to let him know how the filming was going.

Creating a great movie is a difficult thing to do. Mark was learning this as he worked on *Ruff Season*, his short film. Now think about doing this with superstar actors and huge budgets. It takes a director who is a true leader. He has to have imagination, as well as a talent for telling good stories. Not many people have the skill to make all the pieces fit together.

All directors, including Mark, have their own style. It comes through in many of the movies they work on. As Mark has learned, "Give the same script to 10 different directors—you'll get 10 completely different movies."

Quentin Tarantino is a perfect example of a director who has developed his own style. His films include *Pulp Fiction* and *Reservoir Dogs*. Many of his movies have a great deal of violence. His films are known for complicated story lines and interesting conversation. Many of them also contain heart-pounding action.

Steven Spielberg is one of the most famous directors of all time. He has made action films like the *Indiana Jones* series, and intense movies like *Schindler's List*. He's also made films with happy endings, such as *E.T.: The Extra-Terrestrial*. Through it all, his style of directing has been quite unique. He sometimes uses bold lighting, inspiring music, and shots with wide-angle lenses.

These are things the average person usually doesn't think about. It's not only *what* the director shoots, but it's also *how* he shoots it. Have you ever been asked to take a photo of your family or friends? Even if it's just with a camera phone, you still want the best shot possible. You might tell everybody to move in tighter, or remind them to smile. You might tilt the camera or bend down to get the best possible angle. Basically, you are the "director" of that photo.

Mark, using the instincts he's developed as a director, takes a cool photo of himself and his friends. As you can see, he skillfully captured everyone's reflection in the metal bumper of a van.

If that's just for one photo, imagine a whole movie. Remember, a Hollywood studio will be spending millions of dollars on it. Every frame, every shot, and every scene have to be perfect. That's why the director is the most important person on the set.

It all comes down to doing a lot of things at once. Of course, the way the camera shoots the action is very important. Besides that, the actors have to be dressed perfectly. The music has to fit the mood. The background has to seem real. Think about a scene that is taking place in a cold-weather state on a winter day. It *better* look freezing and even snowy.

Because each director has his or her own style, every movie is unique. Martin Scorsese is a true movie business legend. Some of his films are dramatic, violent stories that are set in rough neighborhoods. His movies include *Gangs of New York*, *The Aviator*, *Taxi Driver*, *Raging Bull*, and *Casino*. He is a director who sometimes likes a lot of camera movement. Often times he prefers nonstop action, instead of quick cuts. Music is another important part of a Scorsese movie. He seems to have a skill for picking the right song for the right moment.

Mark is in the process of developing a style all his own. He likes to watch movies and study the work of different directors. By doing that, he learns something new almost every day. "I like shots that are nonstop and move around a lot," Mark says. "Some directors say that zooming in quickly with the camera isn't a good idea. They say that the human eye doesn't follow that type of pattern. I'm not sure I agree, though. I like scenes that show something from far away and then zoom in quickly. I find that interesting to watch on the screen."

Mark keeps a journal about the different movies he watches. That helps him keep everything straight in his mind. He'll describe the plot, the background, and anything else that stands out. This helps him compare the styles of different directors.

Taking notes: Mark studies a film in his living room.

When Mark is asked to choose a favorite director, he doesn't give just one name. Instead, he lists some of Hollywood's most famous ones. He explains why he admires them so much. It's clear that he has spent many hours watching, studying, and learning.

He talks about different scenes and camera angles. For example, Mark mentions the action in Quentin Tarantino's *Kill Bill*. He describes the movie as "amazing." Shaking his head, Mark says, "Tarantino is incredible. I'm inspired by that type of dark comedy. And the way he shoots his action scenes is amazing."

Is Tarantino his favorite director? No, he's just one of many from whom Mark has learned. Mark is totally dedicated. One can only wonder what kind of creative films he will be making in the future. Several years down the road, maybe young filmmakers will be studying *his* work.

Chapter Seven

Following in the Footsteps

Young directors like Mark Mayfield have high hopes and big dreams. They want to follow in the footsteps of the directors that have come before them. In Mark's case, he may even try to be like someone else from Atlanta—Academy Award-winning director Steven Soderbergh. His credits include the *Ocean's Eleven* movies. Those box office smashes feature many of Hollywood's biggest stars. They include George Clooney, Matt Damon, Brad Pitt, Julia Roberts, Andy Garcia, and Don Cheadle.

However, Mark understands something very important. Becoming a big-time Hollywood director isn't the only way to succeed. It's not *only* about creating Academy Award-winning hits. There are many other forms of directing. Many of them pay well and are very exciting.

Let's start with the obvious: television. Every TV show has a director. That's even true with reality shows such as *The Bachelor* and *American Idol.* "Directing a show like *Made* on MTV would be awesome," Mark says. "I wouldn't turn down an opportunity like that."

Television has been an important part of American life for more than 50 years. It all started with the technology itself. The early days featured large and bulky television sets.

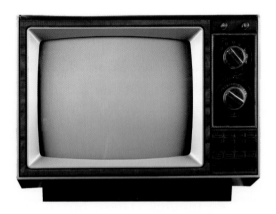

They were far different from the shiny, high-definition flat screens of today. Still, Americans quickly started relying on TV. They watched it for news and information, as well as sports and entertainment.

These days we have hundreds of channels to choose from on sleek, high-definition flat screens.

Years ago, however, only six or seven channels were offered. So, there weren't nearly as many shows, but everybody was watching them. In February of 1983, the final episode of a show called *M*A*S*H* was shown. It became the most-watched television show of all time. Think *American Idol* is popular, with an average of 30 million viewers? That night, for the last episode of *M*A*S*H*, more than 100 million people tuned in!

Anyone would jump at the chance to direct either movies or TV. But that's just the beginning. There are many other things to do, such as directing "independent" films. They are usually called "indie" films (pronounced like the "Indy" 500 car race). These movies are usually made by smaller movie studios. Budgets for indie films are much less than for huge Hollywood movies. That means that large amounts of money aren't available to pay the actors. For that reason, stars normally won't get involved (unless they really love a script).

It's not only a question of money, though. Indie films are usually less mainstream. That means that they only appeal to certain people. Of course, indie filmmakers want their movies to be seen by a big audience. Still, they understand that it's not always possible. There are exceptions, like *The Blair Witch Project*. This independent horror film was released in 1999. Nobody thought it would interest a lot of people. After all, it looked like it was shot with a shaky handheld video camera! Who could have imagined that it would earn more than $100 million? That made it one of the most successful indie films ever.

Besides movies and TV shows, other forms of entertainment also need a director. Music videos come to mind. Most teenagers enjoy watching them, but directing one takes a ton of skill. "Yeah," Mark says, "that would be an interesting challenge. A music video has a lot of quick cutting action. It takes a good director to make it flow with the music just right." That same idea applies to commercials, and even some infomercials (those 30-minute commercials that look like real shows).

A successful director shoots a music video in the heart of Los Angeles.

Think about weddings, bar mitzvahs, and "Sweet 16" birthdays. Many parties will hire someone to film the event. That might not be as big a rush as directing a Matt Damon action movie. Still, this type of work can pay very well. It takes talent and imagination to create something awesome for a family party.

Most directors are skilled with a camera, which can lead to opportunities. As everyone knows, many Americans are interested in celebrities. There are magazines that cover music and movie superstars. All of them feature high-quality photos. An excellent photo of a celebrity can be worth a lot of money. Some of them are taken at concerts and awards shows—and even at restaurants like The Ivy, where photographers wait outside!

It's not just photos that people want to see. They also want information. People want to know how celebrities live and who they are dating! And when celebrities are in trouble with the law, people want to hear all about it. That's why magazines such as *Us Weekly*, *In Touch*, and *People* are so popular. They sell millions of issues each year. More recently, the business of celebrity news has moved online. Web sites such as TMZ.com offer breaking news, photos, and even video. A director who shoots video of a major celebrity can make a good living.

Mark isn't really interested in that type of work, though. He loves the creativity of an actual film. Still, he understands that being a director doesn't mean just one thing. Many readers of this book might be surprised to realize that *they* are directors (or one of their friends, or someone they know at school). That's because of YouTube and other video Web sites. Sure, anybody can shoot something lame and post it on the Internet. These days, however, there are thousands of well-directed videos on YouTube. In some cases, these videos can lead to fame and great rewards.

Take 21-year-old Chris Crocker of Kenwood, Tennessee. Don't know the name? Well, in 2007 a lot of people found out who he was. That's because of a YouTube video he made. In it, he started crying as he asked the world to just "LEAVE BRITNEY ALONE." That was after Britney Spears sang at the 2007 MTV Video Music Awards. Chris' strange YouTube videos have been watched over *10 million times*. That's not all. He was invited to appear on shows hosted by Jimmy Kimmel, Howard Stern, and Ryan Seacrest.

Most people who post videos on YouTube don't receive as much attention as Chris Crocker. Still, shooting and posting videos can be good training for the future. *Killacopter II* is a short film Mark has performed in as an actor. It's posted on YouTube. Mark respects people who use their talents to bring videos to the Internet.

Mark and other actors on the set of *Killacopter II*.

"The world of video is changing," Mark says. "I have my own ideas about what kind of acting and directing I'm interested in. But that's why it's so exciting—everybody is out there doing his own thing. The future should be completely insane."

Chapter Eight

We're All in This Together

A director is an artist ... a person who sees the world through colors, music, backgrounds, and emotions. That describes Mark very well. Go to his house and you'll understand. Mark's room is an expression of his personality. Walk in and almost immediately, you get a sense of who he is.

The walls in Mark's room are forest green. The colors in his bathroom are a nice shade of blue-green. There's a very peaceful, natural feel. "I'm an earth-colored guy who likes the feeling of being surrounded by nature. I always feel myself pulled toward its beauty. That's why many of my stories are inspired by nature."

Mark's desk is placed against the wall across from his bed. His laptop, which sits on it, is open to his Facebook page. This is what connects him to hundreds of friends across the country. The "quotes" section of his page explains his attitude about life. It's a well-known quotation that has been used in many TV shows and movies: "We're all in this together."

Those words mean a lot to Mark. Being a director is a huge responsibility because he's the one in charge. Still, he understands that it's not just about one person. Whether it's a movie, a sports team, or even a family, it's all about teamwork. It's about being there for people and counting on them to be there for you. This is important for Mark because he knows what it's like to feel sad or low.

It's hard to imagine someone like Mark ever feeling blue. After all, he's an honors student who is also a terrific athlete. He's a popular guy who looks forward to a bright future. But Mark is special. Not many teenagers would have the guts to tell other people how they feel. In high school, image counts for so much. It would just be easier to put on a smile and say there's nothing wrong.

Mark cares about people. He knows that many other kids feel down sometimes, too. That's why he's willing to share a little piece of himself. He knows it might make a difference for somebody out there. "I've learned that life has highs and lows," he says softly. "Usually everything is great, but there are times when it seems like life sucks. When I feel like that, I'll go to somebody I trust and open up to them. That's why I have that quote on my Facebook page. It reminds me."

We're all in this together. All of a sudden, those words have a very powerful meaning. It's different for everybody, but Mark's message comes through loud and clear: We all need to reach out sometimes. "Whatever you do," Mark says, "do *something*. Find someone to talk to. It will make a big difference."

These feelings and experiences have definitely helped Mark. They've taught him to be open-minded about things. This starts by understanding that no two people are alike. Our world is made up of all different kinds of people: tall and short, rich and poor, straight and gay, smart (and not as smart!). There are incredible athletes and lousy ones, pretty girls and plain ones, popular and unpopular kids. Mark has learned that it's not about approving of what another person is about. It comes down to accepting people without being cruel, no matter who they are. "Isn't that the way *all of us* want to be treated?" Mark asks.

Many more parts of Mark's room show what he's all about. There's a poster of Middle-Earth that hangs above his bed. It's a tribute to *The Lord of the Rings*. In the bookshelf, there are books such as *The Art of Dramatic Writing*. On the desk, there are magazines with stories about the TV show *Heroes*. Because Mark met the casting director, he's keeping up-to-date with the show.

Below the desk are three locked boxes filled with papers. These are some of Mark's most important things. They contain ideas he has for movies, and a personal journal. Mark has already explained that he likes to keep notes about every movie he sees. He also creates his own original ideas. He writes things down whenever he thinks of them. It might be an idea for a new movie. Or a cool song he hears that might be perfect for a scene he wants to shoot.

One of Mark's ideas is to make a movie about his high school years. This would be very meaningful for him. A lot of other people would probably relate to it as well. "High school is awesome, but it's also really tough in many ways. I think my story might be a film that people will be comforted by. I hope it will help people talk about certain issues that affect high school students," says Mark.

Of course, Mark is not quite ready to make that film. He knows that the final chapter of his high school career hasn't been written yet. But even as it's happening, he'll be writing about it in his personal journal. The world will just have to wait to see it.

One of the more important items in Mark's room hangs over a chair. It's a black jacket that says "New York Film Academy." It would be easy to ignore it, but that would be a mistake. The New York Film Academy means a lot to Mark. Known as "NYFA," this program has played a big part in his life.

Caught in the act! While Mark is at school, Smokey hops online and updates his Facebook page.

It started pretty simply. One night in early 2007, Mark was messing around online after finishing his homework. As usual, he was checking out Web sites about Hollywood and the movie business. He clicked on a link to an organization called the New York Film Academy. What Mark saw blew him away. NYFA had summer programs all over the country for young actors and directors. One of the upcoming programs was being held in Hollywood, at Universal Studios.

It took all of five minutes for Mark to make up his mind. He had been planning to go back to tennis camp for a third straight year. Instead, he asked his parents if he could go to NYFA. His parents have always been very supportive of his interests, so they agreed. They were happy that acting and directing had become so important to him. When Mark had first decided to pursue these activities, they were confused. After all, he had always been quiet and shy. It was a joy to see him chase his dreams and become so outgoing.

In the summer of 2007, Mark boarded a plane and flew to California. When he arrived at Universal Studios, he was excited. He couldn't wait to meet the other high school students who were there. As soon as he did, he knew he was among friends. These were *his* kind of people. They were teenagers from around the country who shared his love of movies. Like him, they wanted to create awesome films. To this day, Mark counts the friends he made at NYFA among his best friends.

Mark learned more that summer than he could have ever dreamed. Something new seemed to happen every single day. The cool thing about NYFA is that they don't just teach. Students actually *make* movies. Everybody is given the opportunity to work on several different short movies. The main thing Mark did was direct his own film, *Ruff Season*. But he also worked on other movies, as an editor, light man, and sound editor. It was like a crash course in all parts of moviemaking.

Mark's summer at NYFA changed his life. He learned so much, and he enjoyed fun times with his new friends. He even did some Hollywood networking—because it was during that trip that he met the casting director of *Heroes*! Amazing things will probably happen to Mark in the future. Still, memories of the summer he spent at NYFA will always stay with him.

Chapter Nine

"Most Likely to Be ..."

People all over the country—and all over the world—love movies. Some of them want to be in the movie business. For those people, Mark Mayfield is an inspiration. In fact, he's a role model for *any* young person who has a dream. Think about it ... this is a teenager who was once afraid to tell people that he wanted to be an actor. Since then, Mark has made much progress. He has become a better actor and director. Even more importantly, he has made progress in his life.

As his high school years went by, Mark's confidence continued to grow. He started looking for ways to do good things for people. In his sophomore year, he did something cool. Midterms were coming up and everyone was studying hard every night. Mark realized that his classmates needed a break. Sometimes it's helpful to just kick back for a little while. After giving it some thought, Mark came up with his idea. He would organize a "movie night" for everyone in his grade.

It seemed simple at first. As it turned out, though, it took a lot of planning. The first thing Mark had to do was find a movie everybody could agree on. This wasn't easy, because each kid had a different opinion. Finally, an agreement was reached: *Batman Begins*. It was a popular choice.

With that out of the way, Mark went to work. He convinced the school to show the movie in the gym. That way, a lot of people could comfortably sit and watch. He also went around to collect money from each kid. Mark and his mom bought pizza, snacks, and drinks. They also went to a store called Party City and bought a popcorn machine.

Sophomore Movie Night was a big hit. Almost 100 people showed up to watch the movie, eat, and hang out. It was very nice to forget about studying for a little while. To this day, people still tell Mark how cool it was that he organized the event.

Mark kept doing things like that, and he also

continued to get excellent grades. Because of every-thing he did, he won an award called the Columbia Book Award. It honors students who do well in school and also have leadership skills. The award was handed out in front of the entire school. Mark had no idea he would win. When the announcement was made, everybody went crazy.

Mark is on a roll. Recently he had the opportu-nity to do some modeling for a line of tennis clothes. He also found a good talent agency in Atlanta to work with him. That might help him get some parts in TV, movies, or commercials. Finally, Mark received some important news. He was accepted to the famous Uni-versity of Southern California. It's known simply as USC. It's also known for being one of the best film schools in the entire country. It has a long list of past students that went on to fame in the movie business.

Mark is thrilled that he will be attending USC. Apparently, Riley is also a proud member of the USC family!

A lot of cool stuff has happened to Mark in the past couple of years. So it's not a surprise that Westminster High gave him another honor. The senior class mentioned him as "Most Likely to Be Famous." Mark feels proud that his friends think of him like that. He definitely plans to "shoot for the stars." Still, Mark is a down-to-earth guy who is on his way to college. He will study hard and get his degree.

We all have hopes and dreams for our future. The directors of tomorrow will probably make movies about it. They will challenge us and inspire us. Mark wants to be one of those people. He thinks big and dreams even bigger. After all, this is the kid who looks outside the window at school sometimes. With his great imagination, he sees villains from whom the world needs saving. It's that unique view of the world that makes him who he is today. Mark may end up on *Heroes*, star in movies, or become a famous director. No matter what, he'll be doing fun and interesting things with his life.

A big thanks to Mark Mayfield and all the dreamers out there. They live in small towns and large cities. Right now, they are in middle school, high school, and college. These creative young people are learning their skills every day. They work behind the camera, and on high school stages. For Mark, the hard work and sacrifice is paying off. He'll soon be on his way to Los Angeles. There, he will someday join a very special club ... the movie business. Hollywood. *The Biz.*